W9-CMO-039

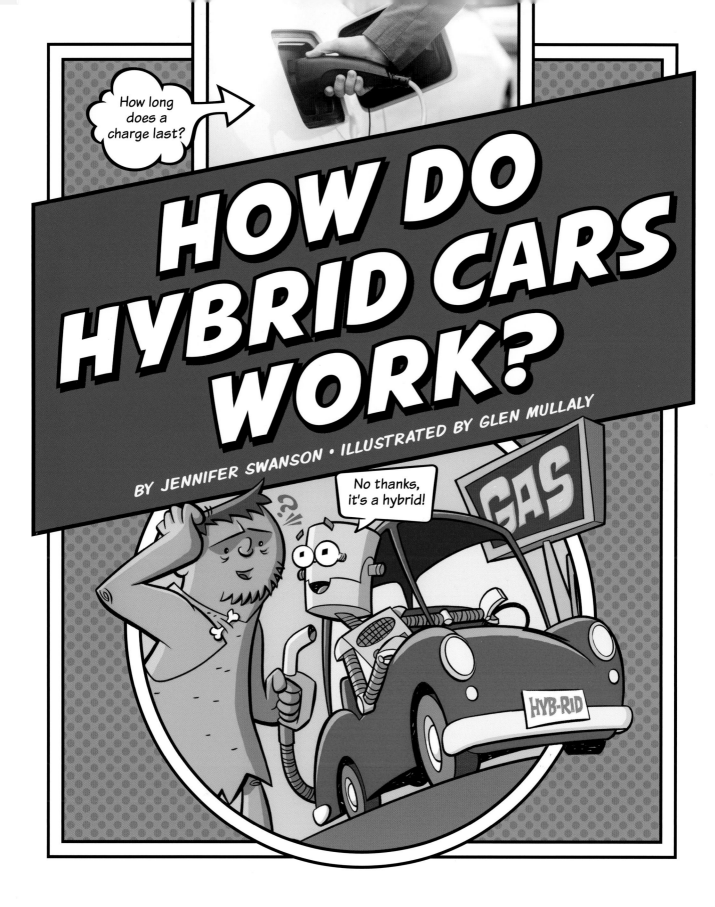

How does this work?

Turn the page to find out!

ABOUT THE AUTHOR

Jennifer Swanson's first love is science, and she is thrilled to be able to combine that with her passion for writing. She has a bachelor of science in chemistry from the US Naval Academy and a master of science in education from Walden University.

ABOUT THE ILLUSTRATOR

Glen Mullaly draws neato pictures for kids of all ages from his swanky studio on the west coast of Canada. He lives with his awesomely understanding wife and their spectacularly indifferent cat. Glen loves old books, magazines, and cartoons, and someday wants to illustrate a book on How Monsters Work!

The Child's World®
childsworld.com

Published by The Child's World®
1980 Lookout Drive • Mankato, MN 56003-1705
800-599-READ • www.childsworld.com

ISBN 9781503855939 (Reinforced Library Binding)
ISBN 9781503856011 (Portable Document Format)
ISBN 9781503856257 (Online Multi-user eBook)
LCCN: 2021939356

Photo Credits © Audio und werbung/Shutterstock.com: 30; Everyonephoto Studio/Shutterstock.com: 16; Friends Stock/Shutterstock.com: cover, 1; Jim Parkin/Shutterstock.com: 26; Mytho88, CC BY-SA 3.0/public domain/via Wikimedia Commons: 6; Nestor Rizhniak/Shutterstock.com: 8; petrmalinak/Shutterstock.com: 14

Printed in the United States of America

TABLE OF CONTENTS

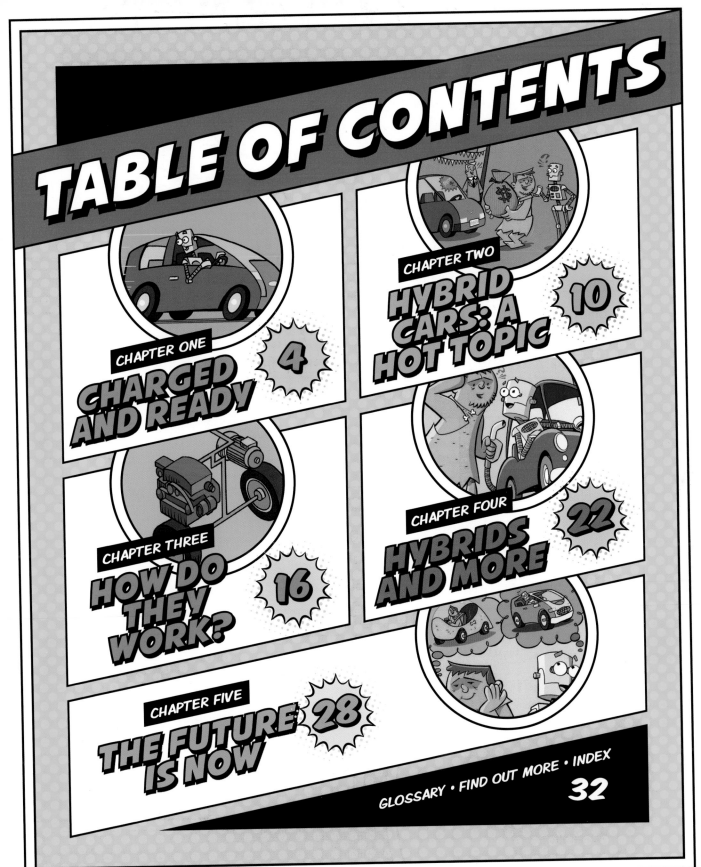

CHAPTER ONE
CHARGED AND READY — 4

CHAPTER TWO
HYBRID CARS: A HOT TOPIC — 10

CHAPTER THREE
HOW DO THEY WORK? — 16

CHAPTER FOUR
HYBRIDS AND MORE — 22

CHAPTER FIVE
THE FUTURE IS NOW — 28

GLOSSARY • FIND OUT MORE • INDEX — 32

CHARGED AND READY

4

"Come on, Mom, let's go!" you shout, diving into the backseat of the car.

You are running late for soccer practice—again. Your mom turns the key.

"Wait a minute!" she says. She runs out and unplugs a thick yellow cord snaking from the car. Back in the driver's seat, she does a quick check. "Battery's charged... plenty of hydrogen in the tank. Let's go!"

"What? Your car needs to be plugged in?" your friend asks as you zip down the street.

"Yup," you declare with pride. "Our car is a hybrid."

A hybrid is a car that can run on two or more different fuel sources—in this case, electricity and hydrogen.

Today, most hybrid cars run on electricity and regular gasoline. These hybrid cars use less gas than regular cars. That means they give off less pollution. Still, carmakers are always looking for new sources of power.

Let's take a look back at the history of hybrid cars.

25 YEARS AGO

Concern about pollution was growing. Hybrid cars had been invented, but they were not yet widely available. Some companies began to make hybrid cars that could be sold to the public. The first such car was the Toyota Prius, which became available in Japan in 1997. Hybrid cars were slow to take off, though. The price was too high for most people.

A 1997 Prius

TIME LINE

1769
The first steam-powered carriage is built in France.

1895
A race is held in France between cars with steam, electric, and gas engines.

1899
In Germany, Porsche develops the very first hybrid car. It teams an electric motor with a gasoline engine.

1908
Henry Ford mass-produces the Model-T, a gas-powered car.

50 YEARS AGO

The rising price of gas created a need for new kinds of cars. In 1969, the GM 12 was developed. The car used electric power when it was traveling slower than 10 miles per hour (18.5 km/h). Then its gas engine kicked in for higher speeds. The car could go up to only 60 miles per hour (97 km/h), though.

120 YEARS AGO

In 1900, the United States had more electric cars on the road than gas-powered ones. Electric cars could travel up to 40 miles (64 km) before their batteries needed to be charged. They sold for $3,000. That was a lot of money back then. Today, it would be like spending $80,000.

1912
The electric starter is invented. Gas-powered cars can now be started with a key instead of a hand crank, and their popularity soars.

1916
Car companies offer hybrid cars that can go up to 35 miles per hour (65 km/h).

1966
Congress recommends using electric cars to cut back on air pollution.

1969
US scientists develop the hybrid-engine design still used today.

Time line continued

BACK TO TODAY

Hybrid cars are becoming more common, even though they are more expensive than regular cars. But engineers are working hard to come up with better, cheaper models, and hybrid sales are going up. They are the cars of the future.

8

Hybrid cars are becoming more popular for buyers.

1991
The US Department of Energy begins developing a "super battery." It can power an electric car longer without being charged.

1997
The Toyota Prius is sold in Japan.

1999
Honda releases the Insight in the United States. It doubles the gas mileage of most cars but can carry only two people.

Time line continued

A STEAMY SOLUTION

The very first cars were powered by steam. Their steam engines had a simple design. Steam was made by heating water in the boiler, a closed container within the engine. The steam turned a rod connected to the wheels. That spun the wheels, making the car go. The more steam, the faster the car went.

Show-off!

2000

The Prius becomes the first four-door hybrid available in the United States.

2011

More than 40 kinds of hybrid vehicles are for sale around the world.

2020

Sales of hybrid cars pass the 17 million mark as demand around the world continues to grow.

CHAPTER TWO

HYBRID CARS: A HOT TOPIC

Hybrid cars are better for Earth than regular cars. But what makes them better, exactly? Well, to answer that question, you need to understand **greenhouse gases**.

But first, imagine walking across a parking lot on a summer day. You see your car glinting up ahead. You open the car door and . . . whew! It's so hot you can barely stand to put your bare legs on the seat. You roll down the windows and wait for the car to cool off.

Why is your car so much hotter than the air outside, anyway? It's because of the windows. The sun's rays stream through the glass, but the heat can't escape back out. The windows trap heat inside the car.

Greenhouse gases are way up in the sky, but they work the same way as those car windows. They trap heat inside Earth's atmosphere. Usually, being warm is a good thing, right? But nobody wants to be too warm. Unlike you, Earth can't just roll down the windows when it gets too hot.

Instead, as greenhouse gases increase, the planet's temperature slowly begins to rise. This is called **global warming**, and it can be pretty scary to think about. Global warming has been linked to all kinds of problems, from natural disasters and disease to animals dying off.

But what does all this have to do with hybrid cars? Well, burning gasoline gives off greenhouse gases. Regular cars are one of the major causes of global warming. Hybrid cars use less gasoline, so they contribute less to global warming.

WHO NEEDS 'EM? WE DO!

Hybrid cars have several benefits. Take a look:

1. They use less gasoline. That means drivers spend less money on gas.

2. Less gas means fewer oil wells. Oil wells can lead to oil spills. They harm wildlife, too, so the fewer the better.

3. The United States has to buy a lot of its oil from foreign countries. And this comes with a whole host of political problems. Less gas means we don't have to rely so much on foreign oil.

4. Hybrid cars work just as well as gasoline-powered cars, and they are quieter.

5. And the best reason—hybrid cars give off fewer greenhouse gases.

A High Price

So why isn't everyone driving a hybrid? The biggest answer is price. A new hybrid car still costs about $5,000 more than a regular car. And used hybrid cars are hard to find.

However, to offset the cost, the US government has offered a discount on taxes to people who own a hybrid. Plus, hybrid owners will definitely spend less time and money at the gas pump. They can save hundreds of dollars a year on gas.

For many, though, the benefits do not yet outweigh the cost. As automakers keep working on new and better models, the prices will come down. Who knows how cheap a hybrid will be by the time you're ready to buy one?

It's worth it.

CHAPTER THREE

HOW DO THEY WORK?

A hybrid car can go just as far and just as fast as a regular car. How does it perform as well with less gas? Let's use the example of the most common type, the hybrid-electric vehicle, or **HEV**. It still has a gas engine.

However, this engine is much smaller than in a regular car. It doesn't have to be as powerful because it gets help from an electric motor with a rechargeable battery. The car is constantly switching between the gas engine and the electric motor. Its onboard computer makes sure everything happens smoothly.

THREE WAYS AN HEV SAVES GAS

Electric Motor

Gas Engine

Battery

1. The electric motor runs the car by itself at low speeds. It also provides energy to the gas engine when the car needs it most. The electric motor gives an extra push when the car is speeding up or going uphill.

2. Every bit of energy is saved. While the car is running, extra energy from the electric motor and the gas engine are stored in the battery.

3. At very low speeds, or when the car is sitting still at a stoplight, it only uses energy from the battery.

GIVE ME A BREAK!

Did you know that slowing a car down means losing energy? People at Toyota wanted to save that energy. So they developed a special kind of brake system that traps that energy and stores it in the battery for later use. More gasoline is saved.

STOP WASTING ENERGY!

BATTERY TALK

Hybrid cars have batteries that weigh about 120 pounds (54 kg). They fit behind the backseat or under the trunk and can last up to 120,000 miles (200,000 km).

Scientists hope to soon replace these batteries with the same kind found in cell phones or laptops. These batteries are extremely light and powerful, and they would work better. Maybe one day, if your car runs out of power, you'll pop open your cell phone and put its battery in your engine!

Light and Sleek

Which do you think takes more energy: moving something heavy or moving something light? If you guessed "heavy," you're right! That's why hybrid cars are made to be as light as possible.

Hybrid cars are also sleek. They are designed to create very little **wind resistance**. Imagine riding your bike and sitting up tall. You can feel the air pushing on the entire upper part of your body. This is wind resistance. The air slows you down, and you have to pump harder to go as fast as you'd like to. Now imagine

No fair! I can't bend very well!

leaning over the handlebars and bending your back. Most of the air glides right over your back. With less wind resistance, you don't have to pedal as hard.

Hybrid cars are designed with this in mind. The edges are rounded and the top is a smooth curve, so they catch as little wind as possible. That means they can go faster with less power and—you guessed it—less gas.

LIGHTER = FASTER

A hybrid engine isn't as powerful as a regular gas engine. But does that mean it's slower? Nope. Hybrid cars make up for the difference by using lighter materials. Automakers use aluminum or carbon fibers when making hybrid cars. These are a lot lighter than the heavy metals used in regular cars.

CHAPTER FOUR

HYBRIDS AND MORE

Usually, when people say "hybrid," they mean HEV. However, there's recently been a new twist on the old model.

Plug It In

Add a P to HEV and what do you get? The plug-in hybrid electric vehicle (PHEV)! This up-and-coming hybrid is basically an HEV with an extension cord. An HEV owner only has one way to fuel up—at the gas pump. But a PHEV owner has two options—the gas pump or an electrical outlet.

A PHEV can be plugged in at night, and in the morning, it's ready to go. The car can run on its battery without using any gas for up to 40 miles (64 km).

That's less than many people drive in a day. So, as long as you plug it in at night, you could drive the car for weeks without using any gas. But don't worry if you drive too far. The gasoline engine kicks in when the car needs more energy.

Diesel Anyone?

HEVs are the greenest cars on the road. But engineers have also developed cars that run on alternative fuels. The goal is still the same—to burn less gas.

A clean diesel car is one such option. It runs on diesel fuel. Like gasoline, diesel comes from oil wells. However, diesel is more powerful. Gallon per gallon, it contains 10 percent more energy than regular gasoline.

The diesel engine is also key. Though it looks a lot like a regular gas engine, this engine uses a much higher pressure and temperature. This makes the car run farther on less fuel. And that means fewer greenhouse gases. The big drawback of the diesel car is that it creates smog—a fog filled with stinky pollution.

Soybeans to the Rescue

Scientists have looked for ways to make diesel fuel that doesn't cause smog. Surprisingly, they found their answer in a soybean field. **Biodiesel** fuel is made from soybean oil, and it burns clean.

It sounds like a perfect solution, doesn't it? Not exactly. Biodiesel provides less energy than gasoline. That means you need more of it to go the same distance. It is also difficult to store. If you keep biodiesel fuel around too long, it starts to form clumps. Any clumps in the liquid can cause problems for the engine.

CORN ON THE CAR?

Another type of fuel for cars is ethanol. Made from corn and other plants, ethanol is renewable. This means that we can make more of it. As long as we grow corn, we can have ethanol. And cars that burn ethanol produce 30 percent fewer greenhouse gases than regular cars. E85 is the most common ethanol-based fuel. It is made up of 85 percent ethanol and 15 percent regular gasoline. The problem is that E85 isn't easy to find in every region. What happens if you take a road trip to an area that doesn't have it? This fuel also isn't as powerful as gasoline.

An ethanol plant converts corn into fuel.

POPULAR HYBRID CARS

Toyota Prius

Honda Insight

Chevrolet Bolt

Ford Fusion Hybrid

CHAPTER FIVE

THE FUTURE IS NOW

What is the future of green, clean-burning cars? HEVs have taken us halfway there. But what if we didn't need gasoline at all? Engineers are developing such a car. Instead of gasoline, this car runs on hydrogen gas. (That's gas like air, not liquid gasoline.) Each car contains a device called a **fuel cell**. It can use the hydrogen to make electricity. Let's take a closer look.

1. The electric motor powers the car. It is much quieter than a regular engine and doesn't need as many repairs.

2. The power control unit makes sure electricity goes where it is needed.

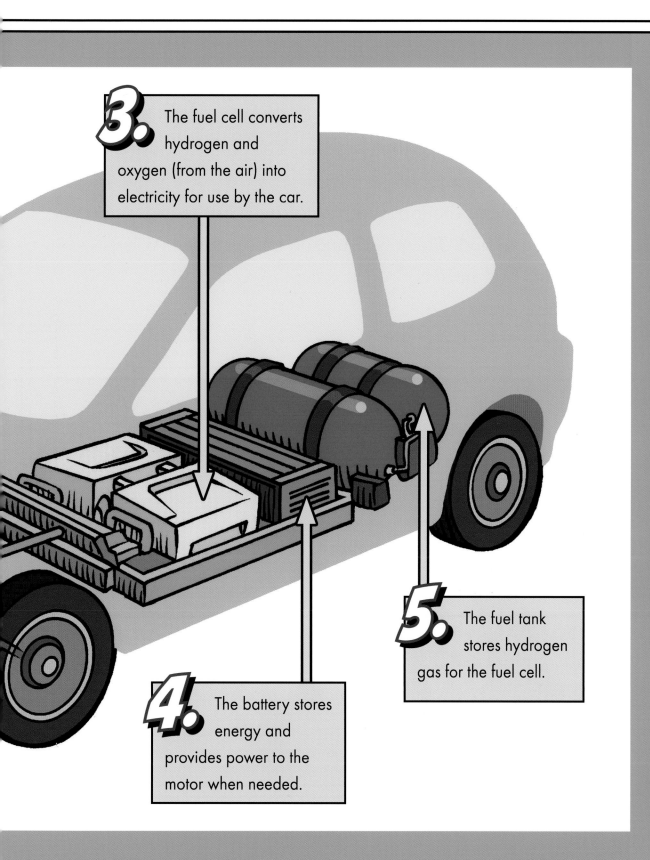

3. The fuel cell converts hydrogen and oxygen (from the air) into electricity for use by the car.

4. The battery stores energy and provides power to the motor when needed.

5. The fuel tank stores hydrogen gas for the fuel cell.

The best part is that this car is clean burning. It does not give off any greenhouse gases. The only exhaust that comes out is water.

A problem, though, is that hydrogen gas stations are not easy to find. There isn't one on every corner. At least, not yet. And since hydrogen is explosive, a gas leak could be dangerous.

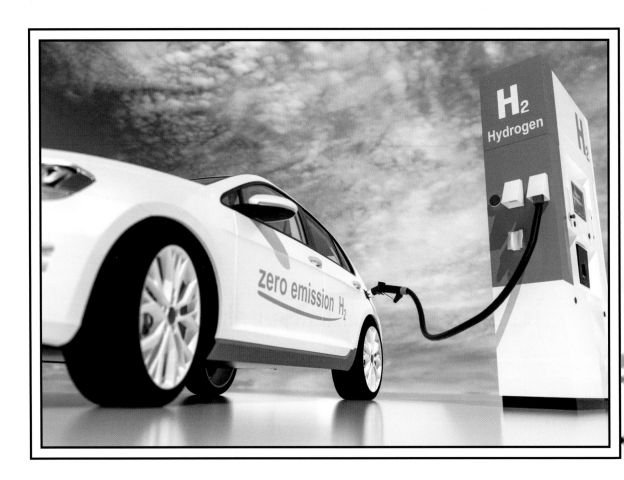

What Will You Be Driving?

Experts predict that the sale of hybrids and other fuel-efficient cars will keep rising. And drivers will have better and better models to pick from in the future. Automakers are now experimenting with a car that runs on solar energy. Panels on the roof would gather energy from the sun and funnel it to the engine. Cool, huh? Who knows what you'll be driving!

GLOSSARY

biodiesel (by-oh-DEE-zuhl): Biodiesel is a fuel made from soybeans and other plants. Biodiesel is a fuel for cars that gives off less pollution than gasoline.

fuel cell (FYOO-uhl SEL): A fuel cell is a device that makes electricity from a chemical reaction. Future cars could be powered by fuel cells that make electricity from hydrogen and oxygen.

global warming (GLOH-buhl WARM-ing): Global warming is the increase in Earth's average temperature. Burning gasoline causes global warming.

greenhouse gases (GREEN-hows GAS-iz): Greenhouse gases are gases in Earth's atmosphere that trap heat from the sun. Scientists believe that increasing greenhouse gases are causing global warming.

HEV: HEV stands for hybrid-electric vehicle. An HEV is a hybrid that has both a gas engine and an electric motor.

wind resistance (WIHND rih-ZIHS-tuhns): Wind resistance is the force of air on a moving object. Hybrid cars are designed to reduce wind resistance.

FIND OUT MORE

Visit our website for links about how hybrid cars work:
childsworld.com/links

Note to Parents, Teachers, Caregivers, and Librarians: We routinely verify our Web links to make sure they're safe and active sites. So encourage your readers to check them out!

INDEX

biodiesel, 25
boiler, 9
brake system, 19
diesel fuel, 25
electric motor, 17, 18, 28
electricity, 4, 28–29
ethanol, 26
fuel cell, 28–29

gas engine, 7, 16–18, 21, 25
gasoline, 5, 12, 14, 19, 23, 25, 26, 28
global warming, 12
greenhouse gases, 10–12, 14, 25, 26, 30
hybrid-electric vehicle (HEV), 16, 18, 22, 24, 28

hybrid engine, 21
hydrogen, 4, 28–29, 30
oil wells, 14, 25
plug-in hybrid-electric vehicle (PHEV), 22–23
rechargeable battery, 17
steam, 9
wind resistance, 20–21